PORTRAITS TO COLOR
ADULT COLORING ADVENTURE IN GRAYSCALE

18 GRAYSCALE DESIGNS

©2020 TWISTED BRANCH STUDIOS
ALL RIGHTS RESERVED.
NO PORTION OF THIS BOOK MAY BE REPRODUCED
OR DISTRIBUTED WITHOUT THE
WRITTEN CONSENT OF PUBLISHER & ARTIST.

ISBN: 9798653511837

Publisher: Twisted Branch Studios

ILLUSTRATOR: CYNTHIA KLOETER

FEATURED COLORING ARTIST: KAREN SENERCHIA

TwistedBranchStudios@gmail.com

Artisan Raw Hand Drawn Illustrations

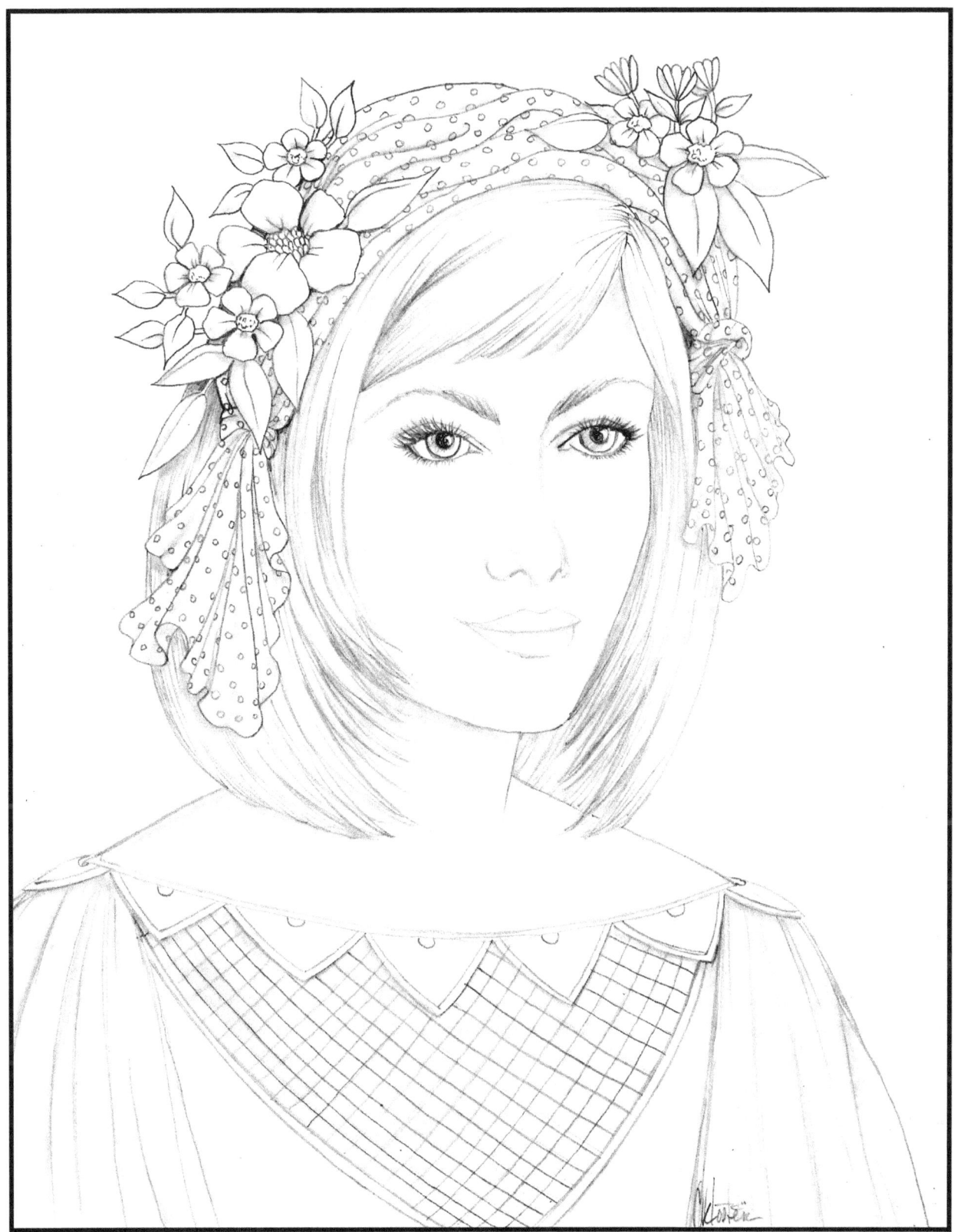
©Twisted Branch Studios

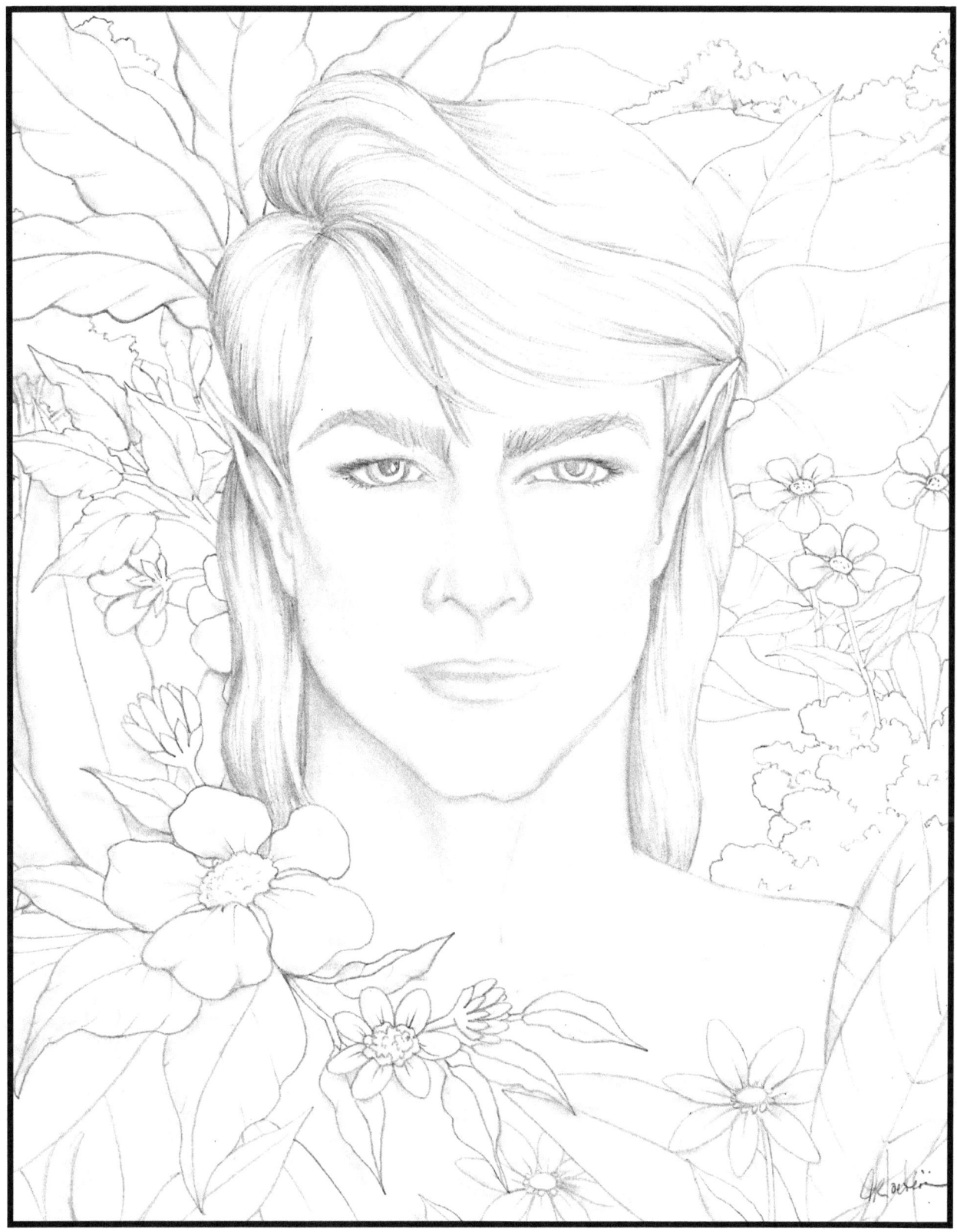

©Twisted Branch Studios

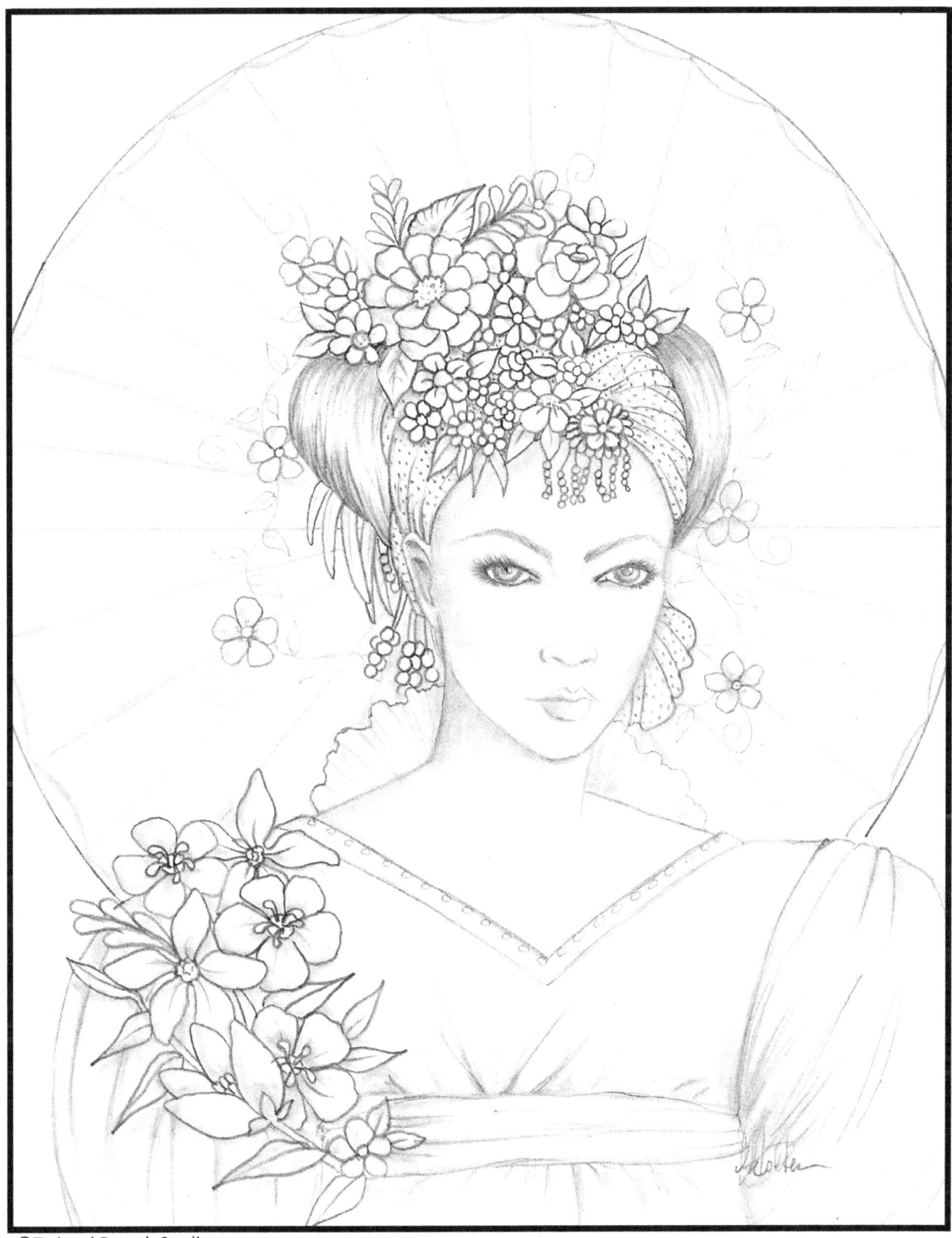

©Twisted Branch Studios

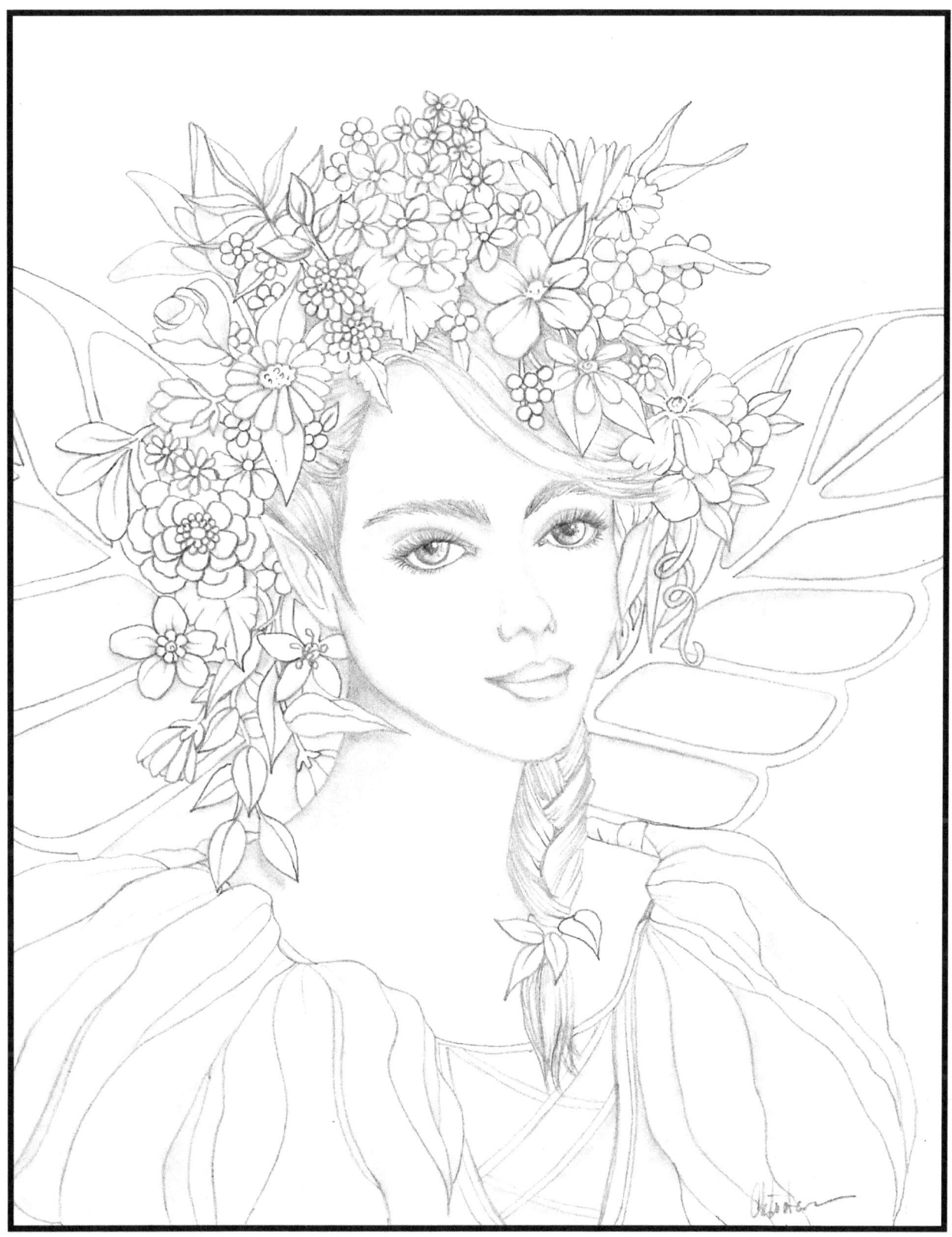
©Twisted Branch Studios

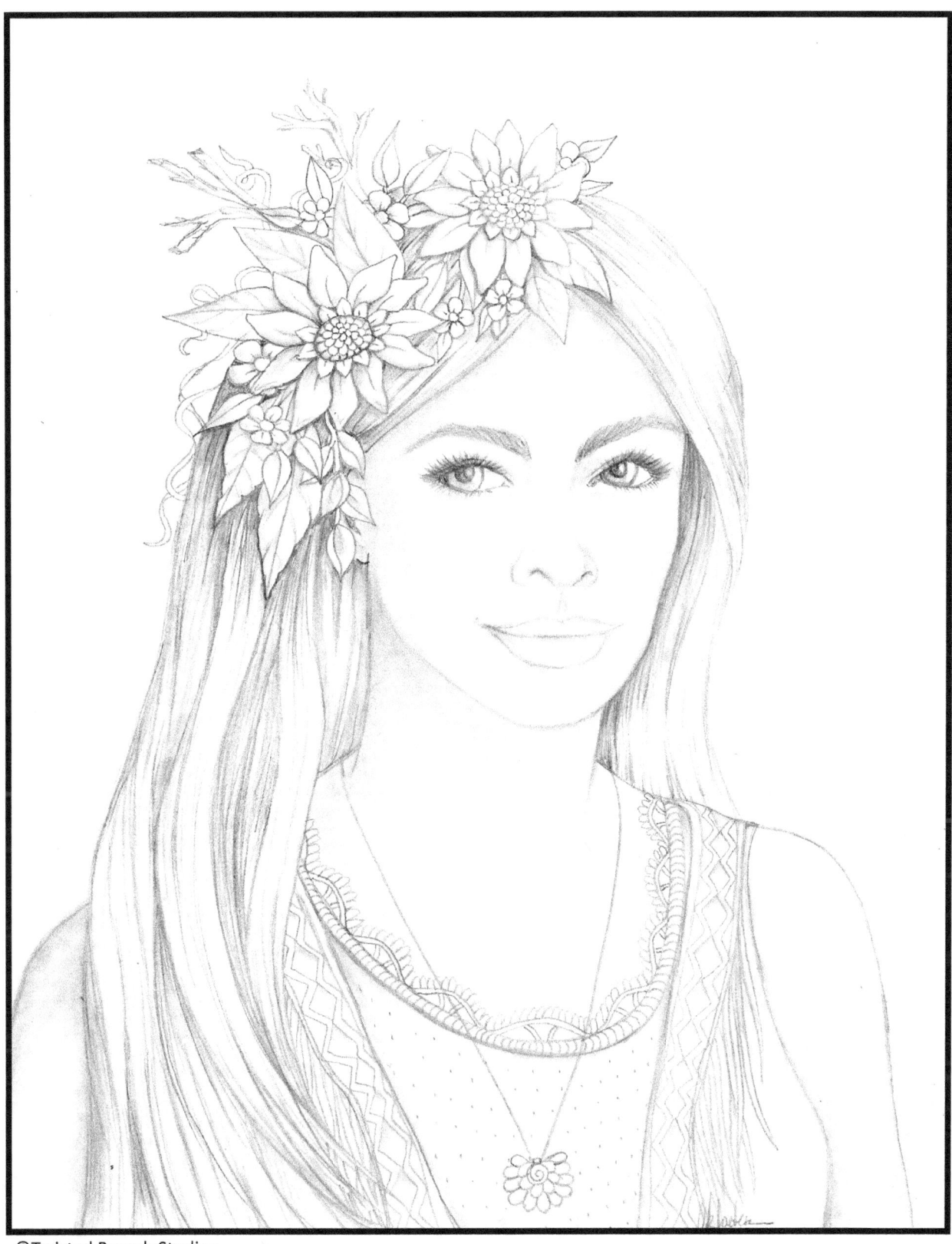

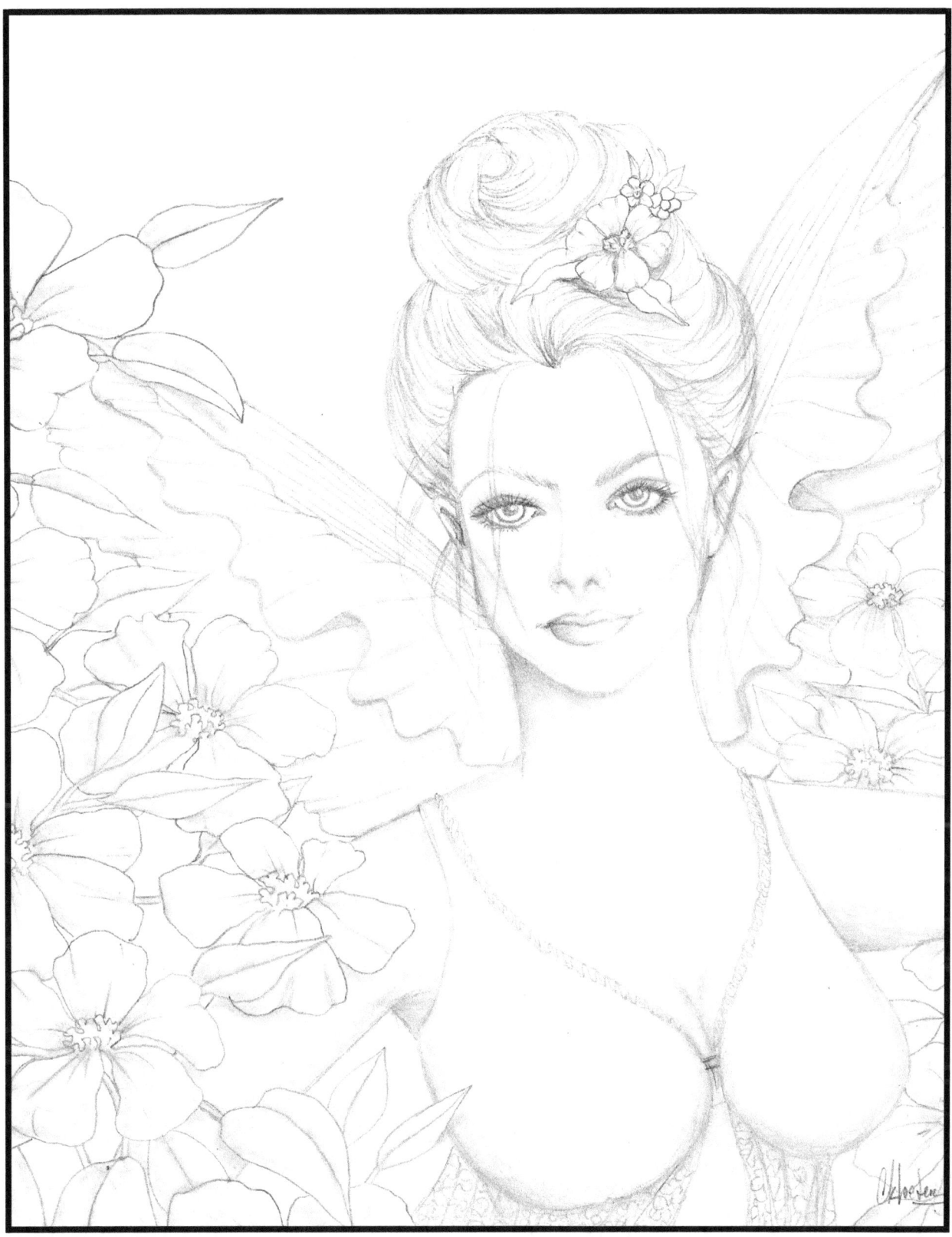

©Twisted Branch Studios

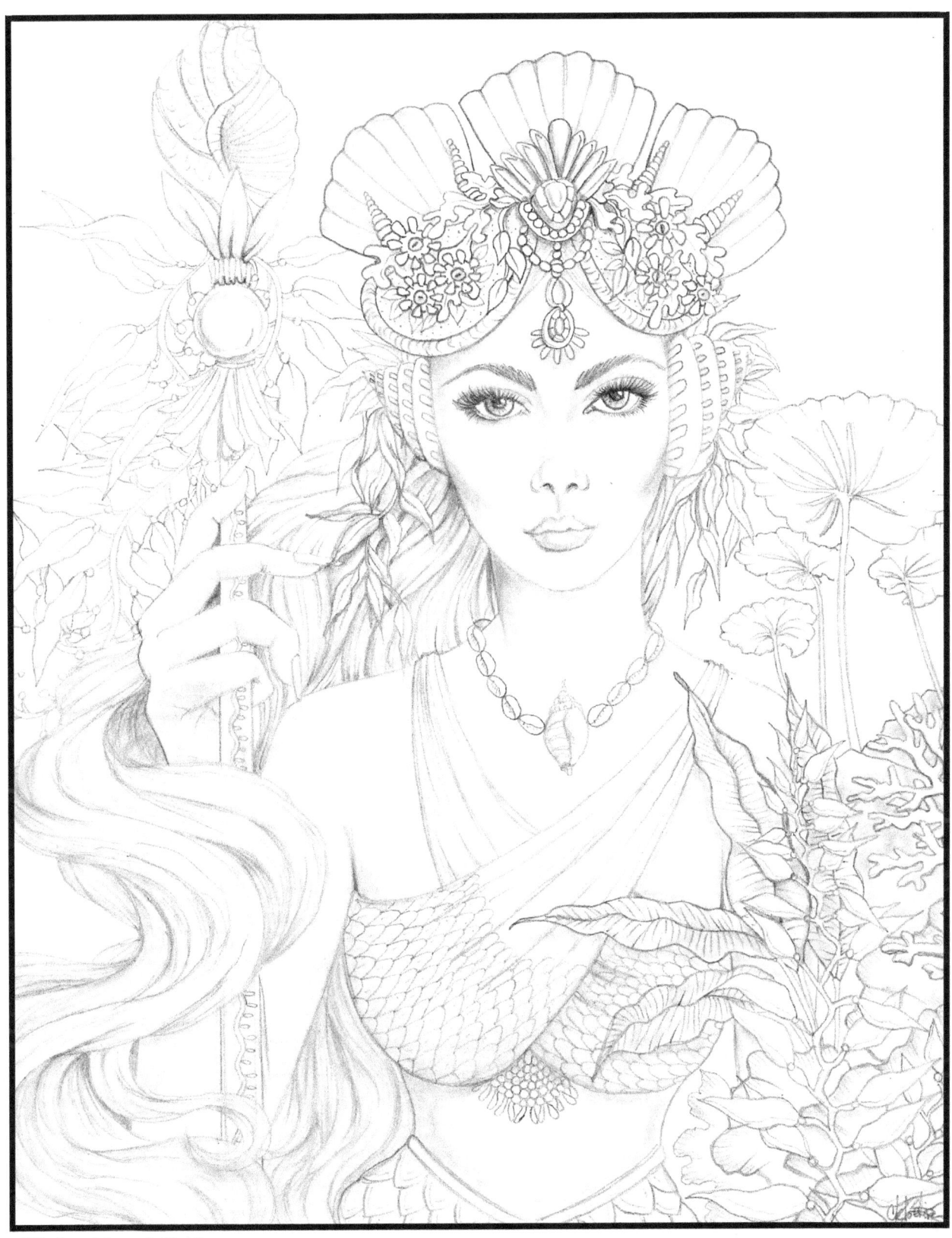

©Twisted Branch Studios

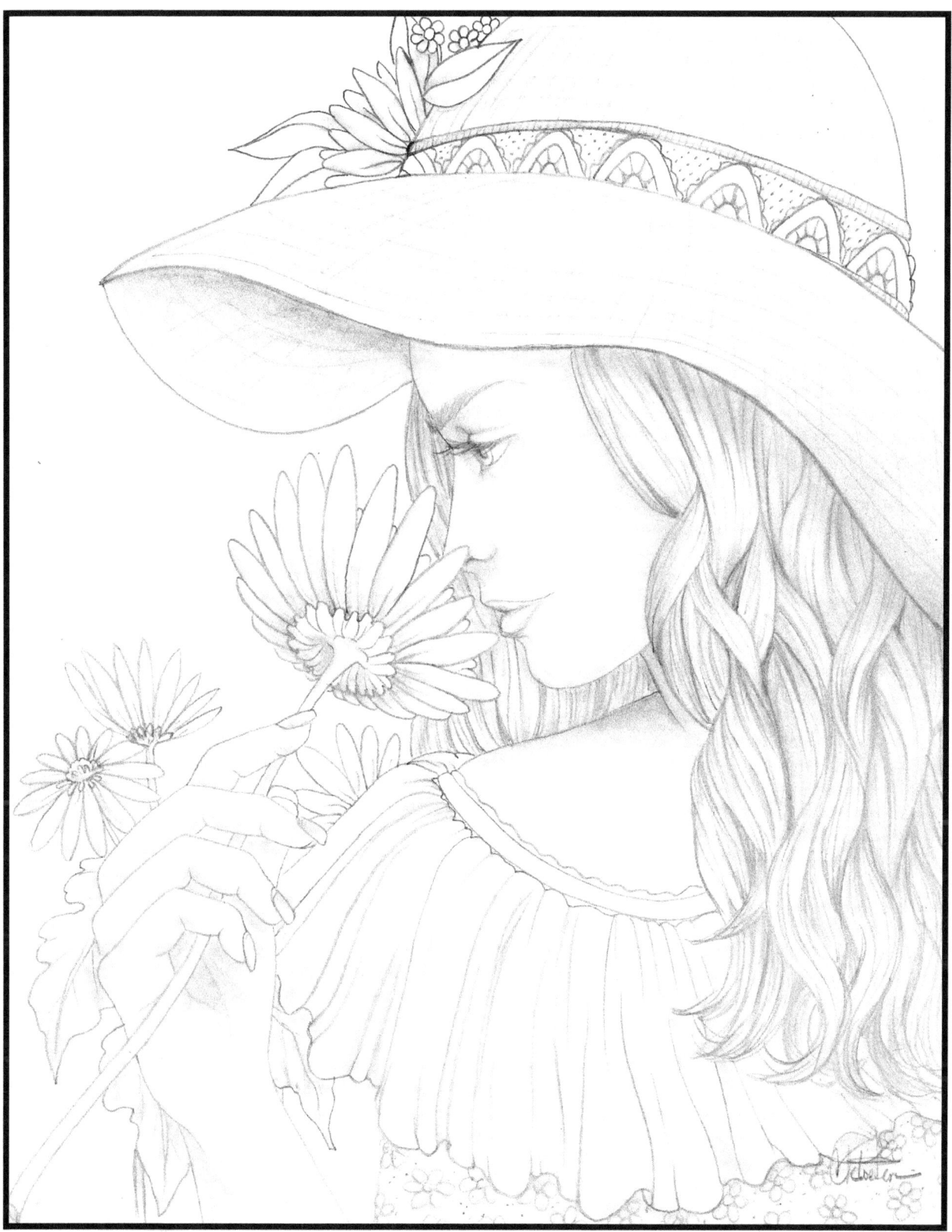

©Twisted Branch Studios

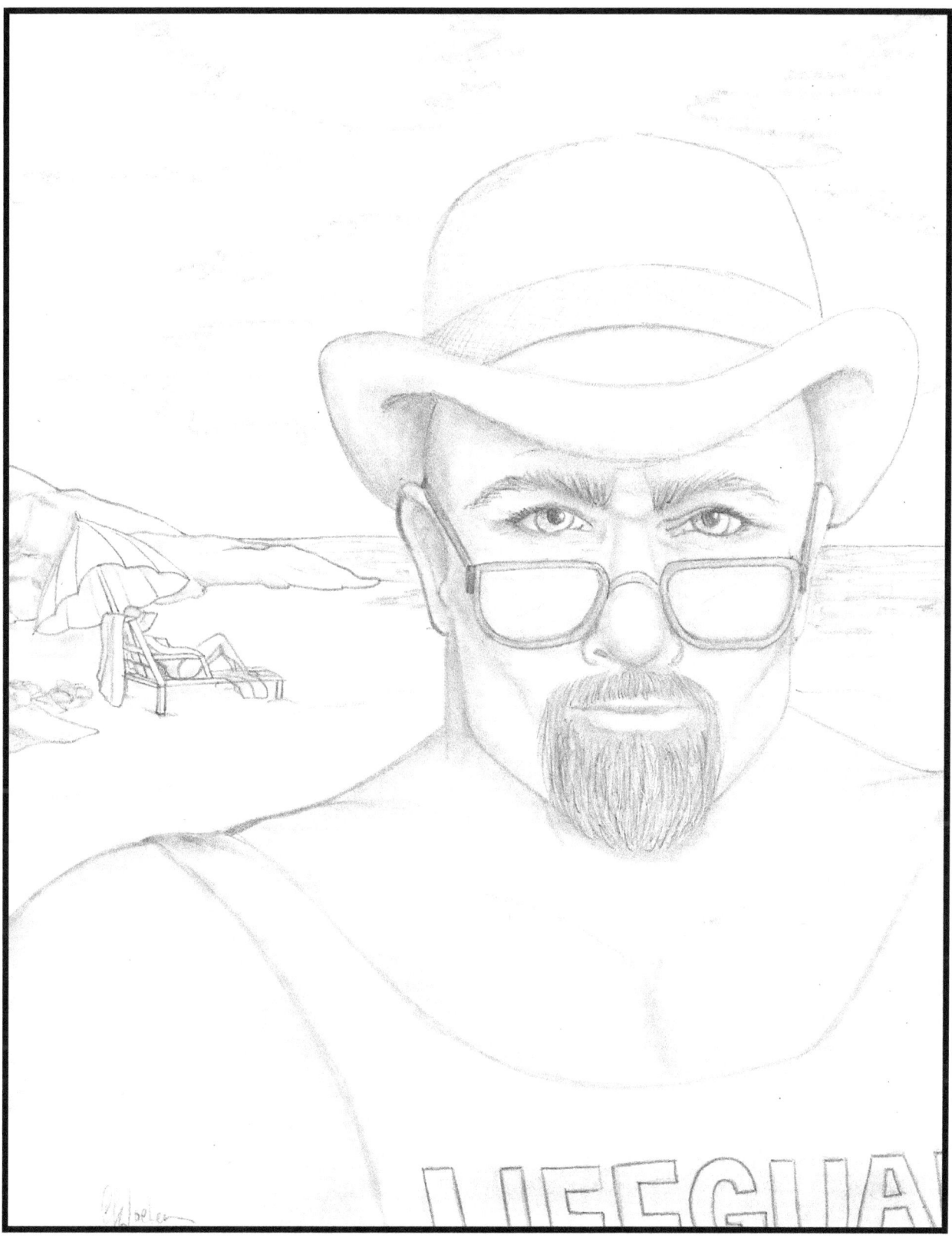

©Twisted Branch Studios

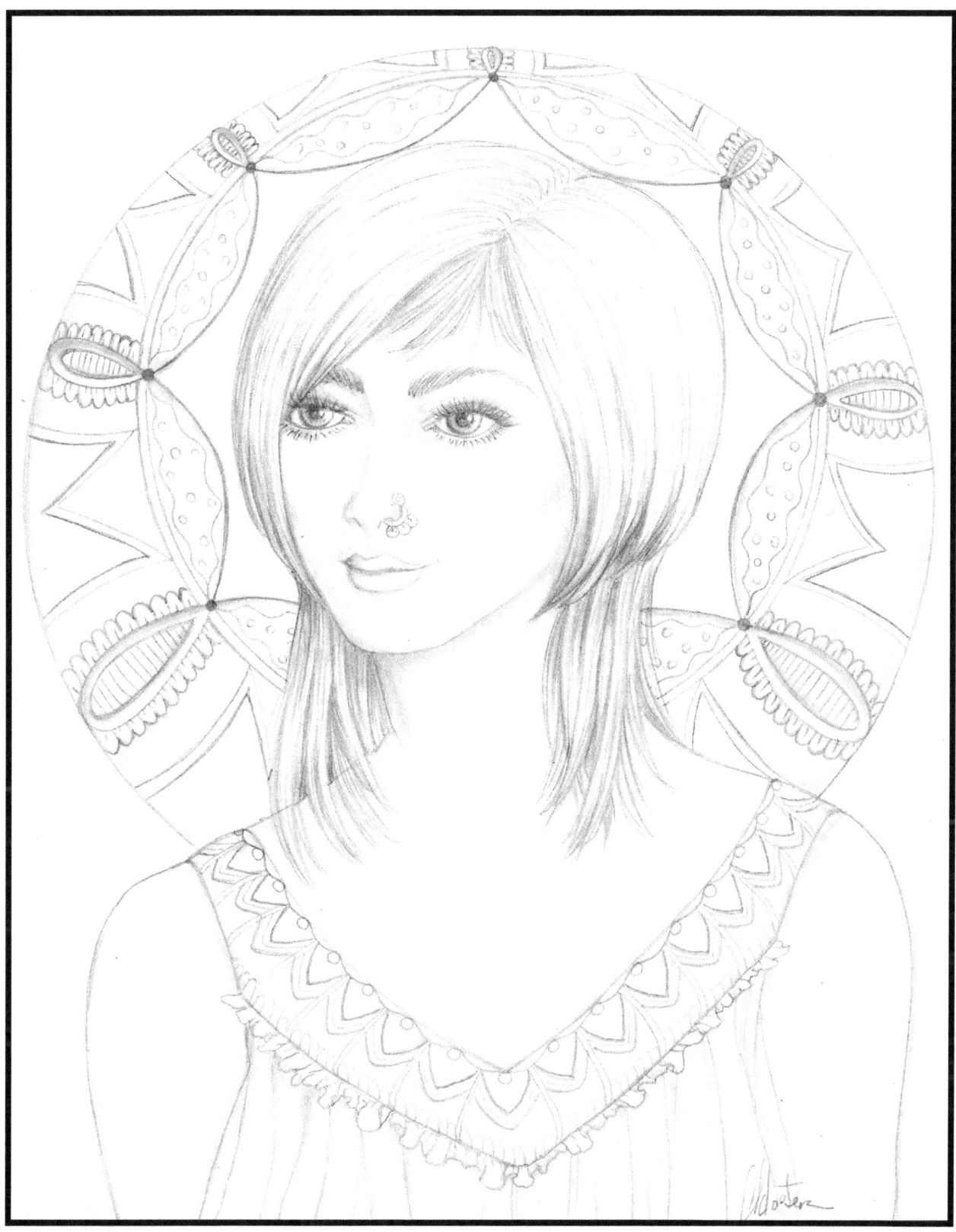
©Twisted Branch Studios

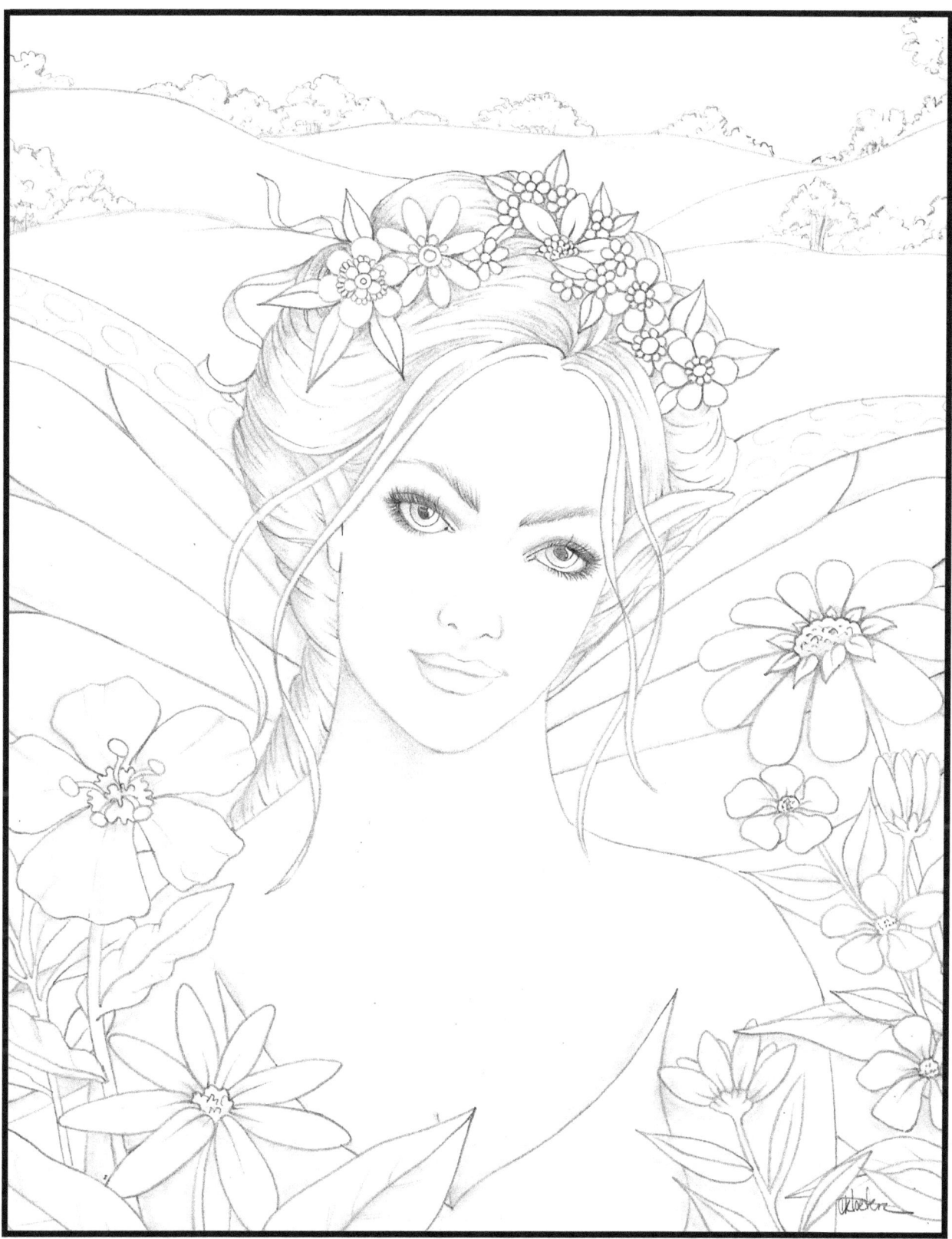
©Twisted Branch Studios

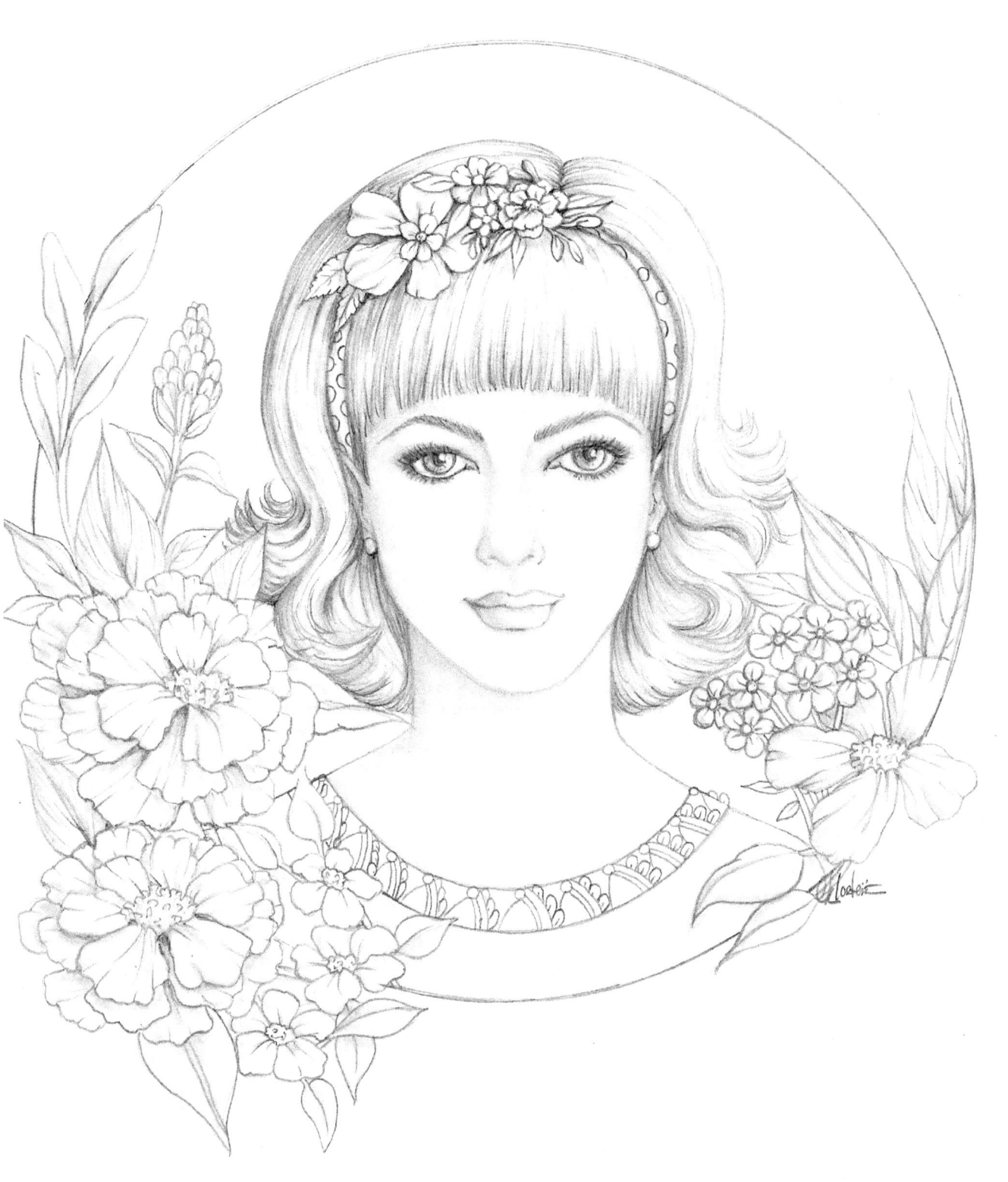

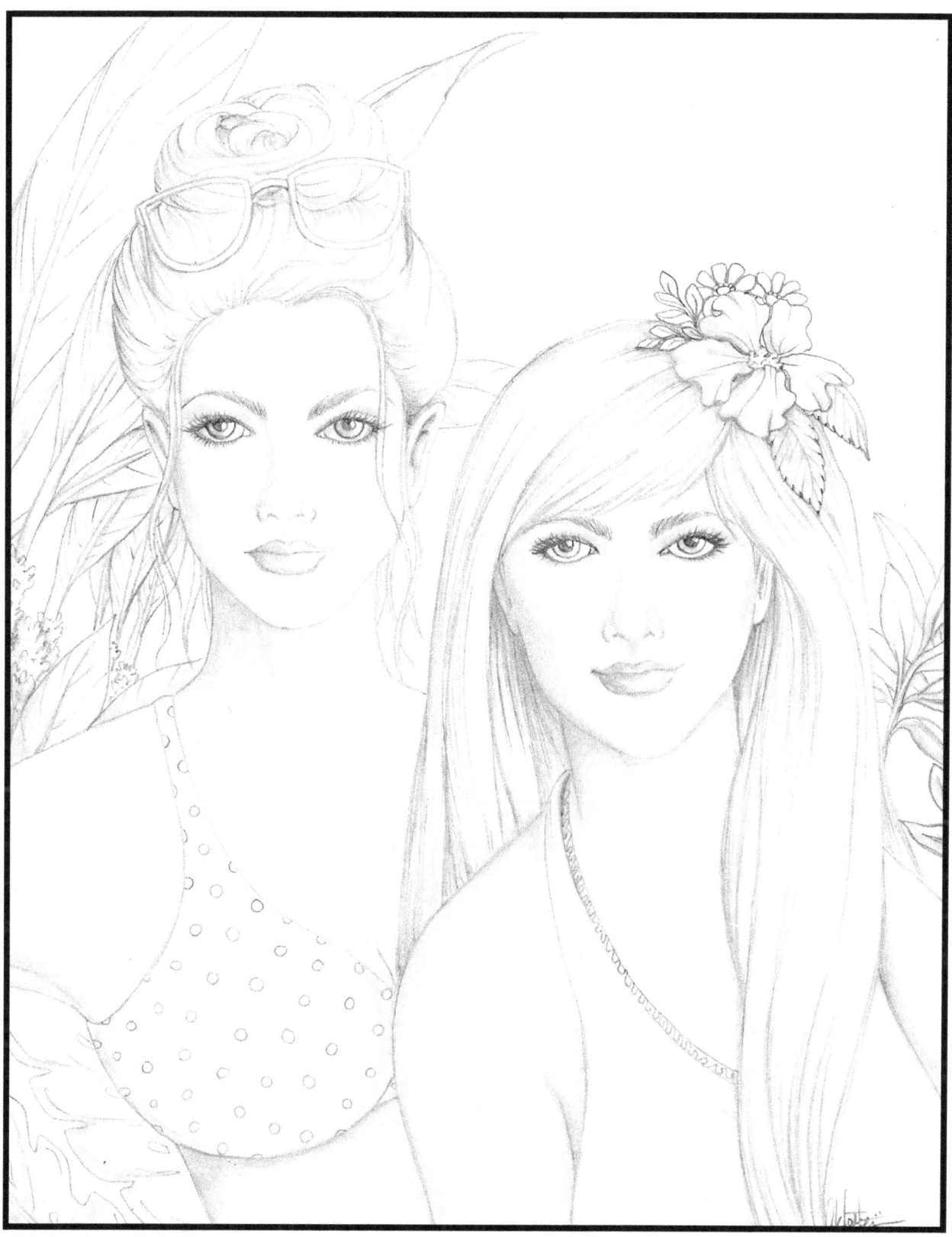

©Twisted Branch Studios

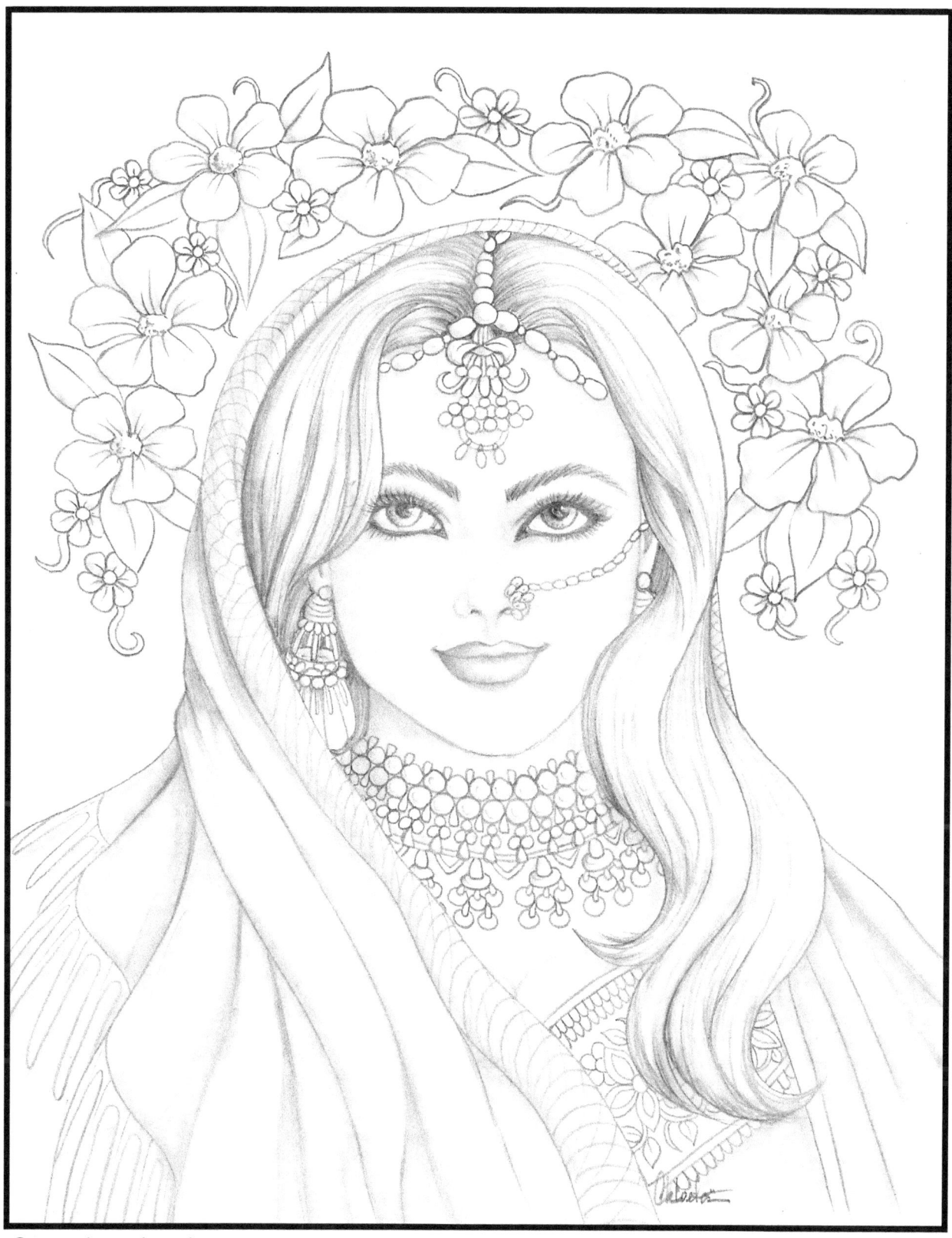

©Twisted Branch Studios

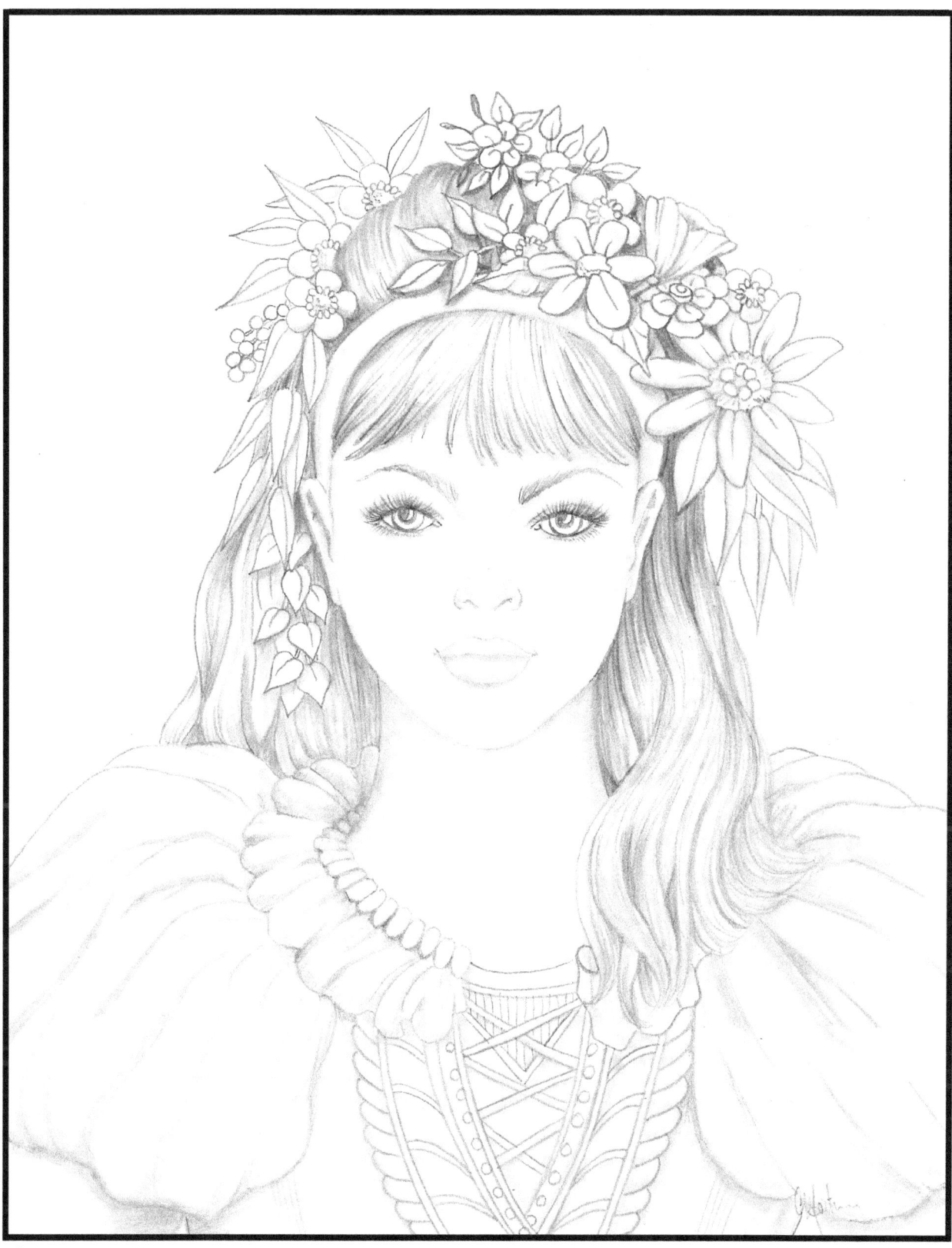

©Twisted Branch Studios

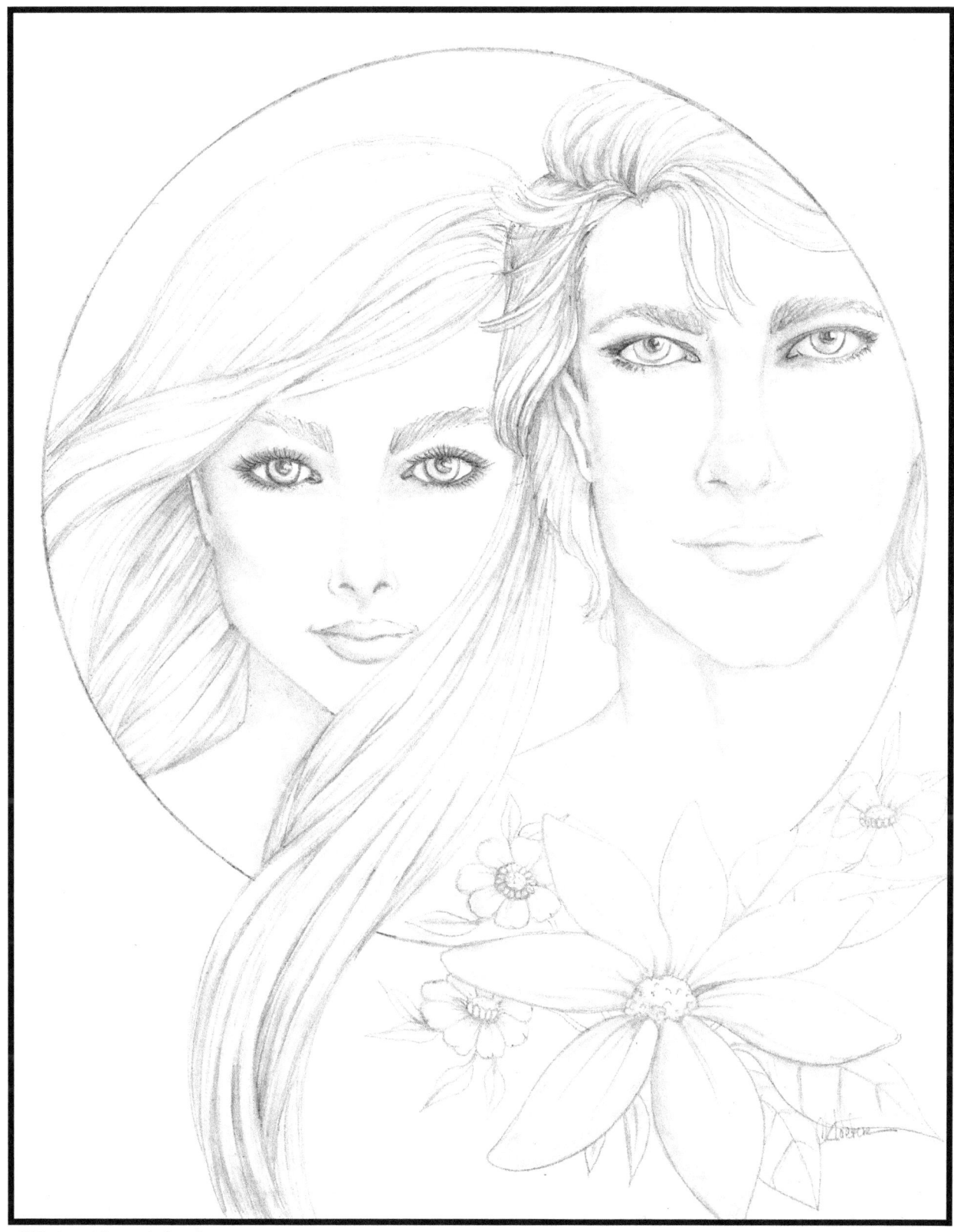

©Twisted Branch Studios

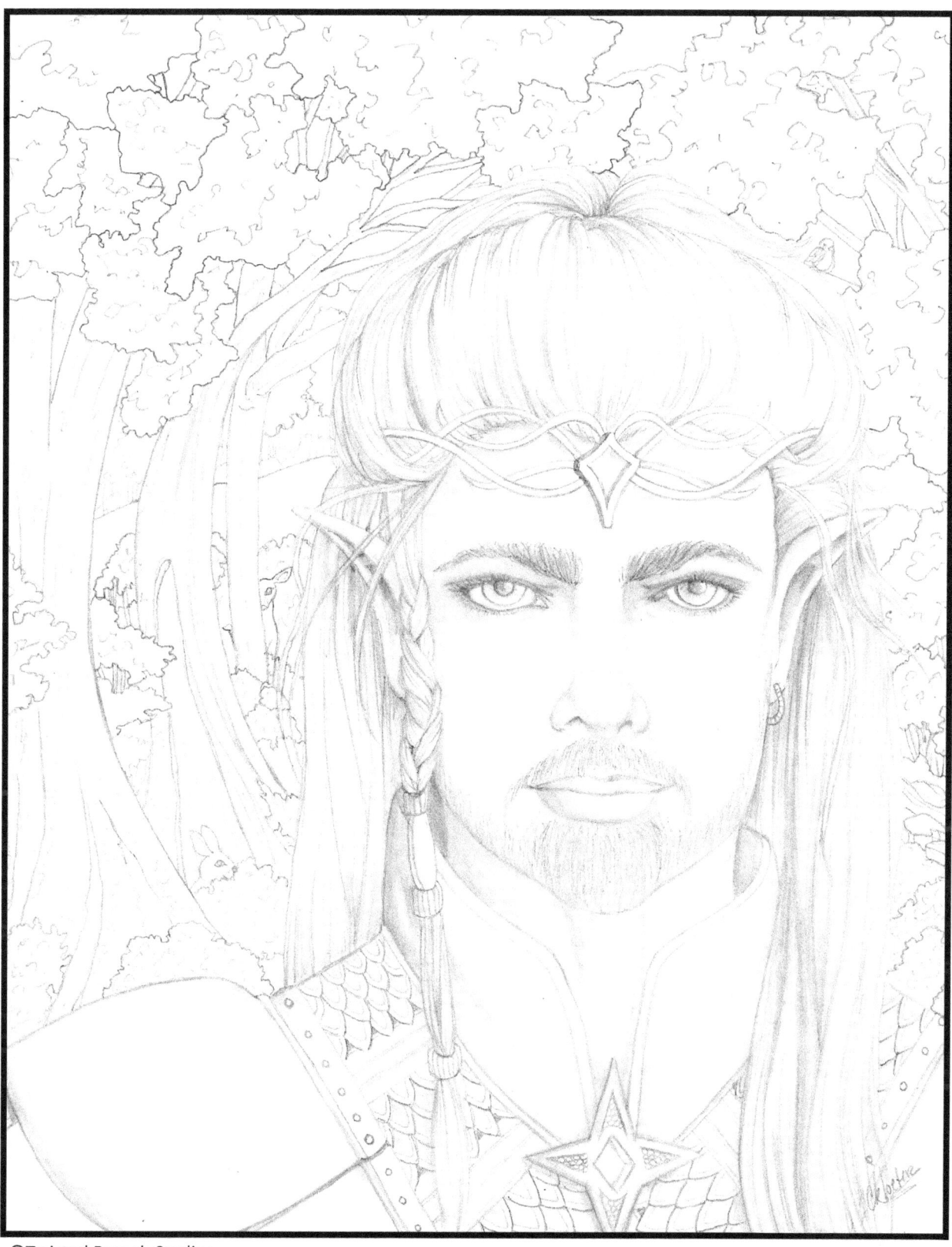

©Twisted Branch Studios

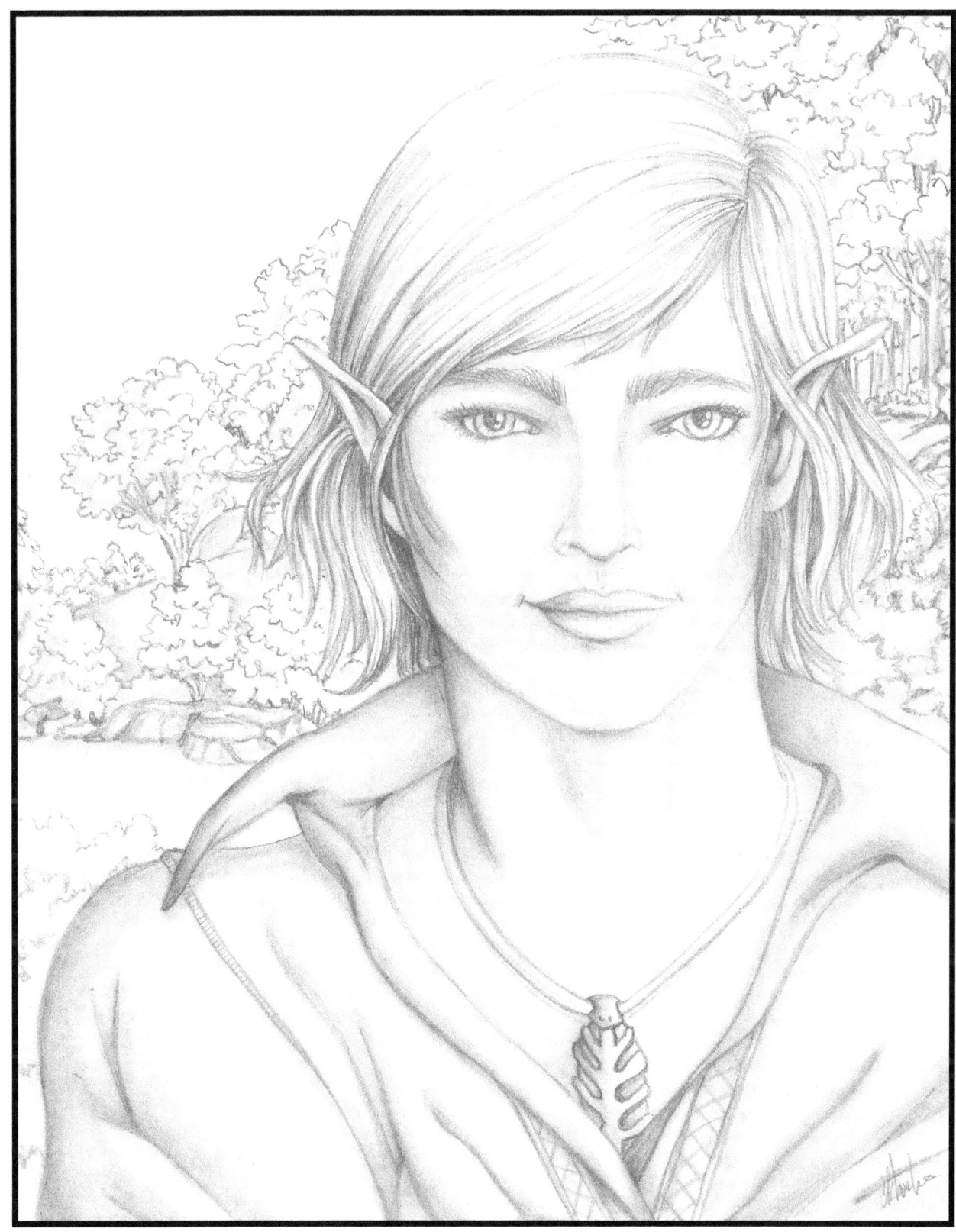

©Twisted Branch Studios

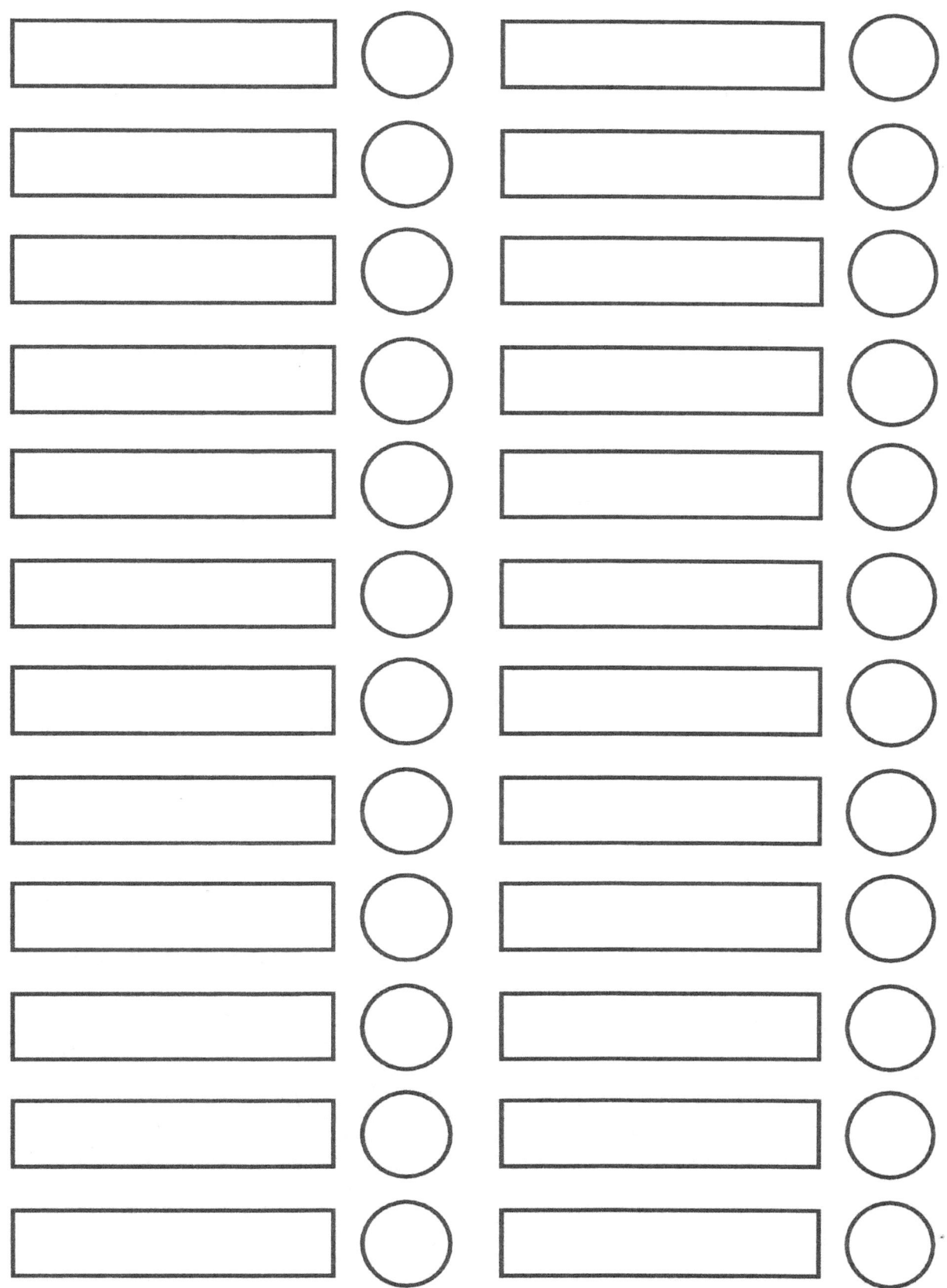

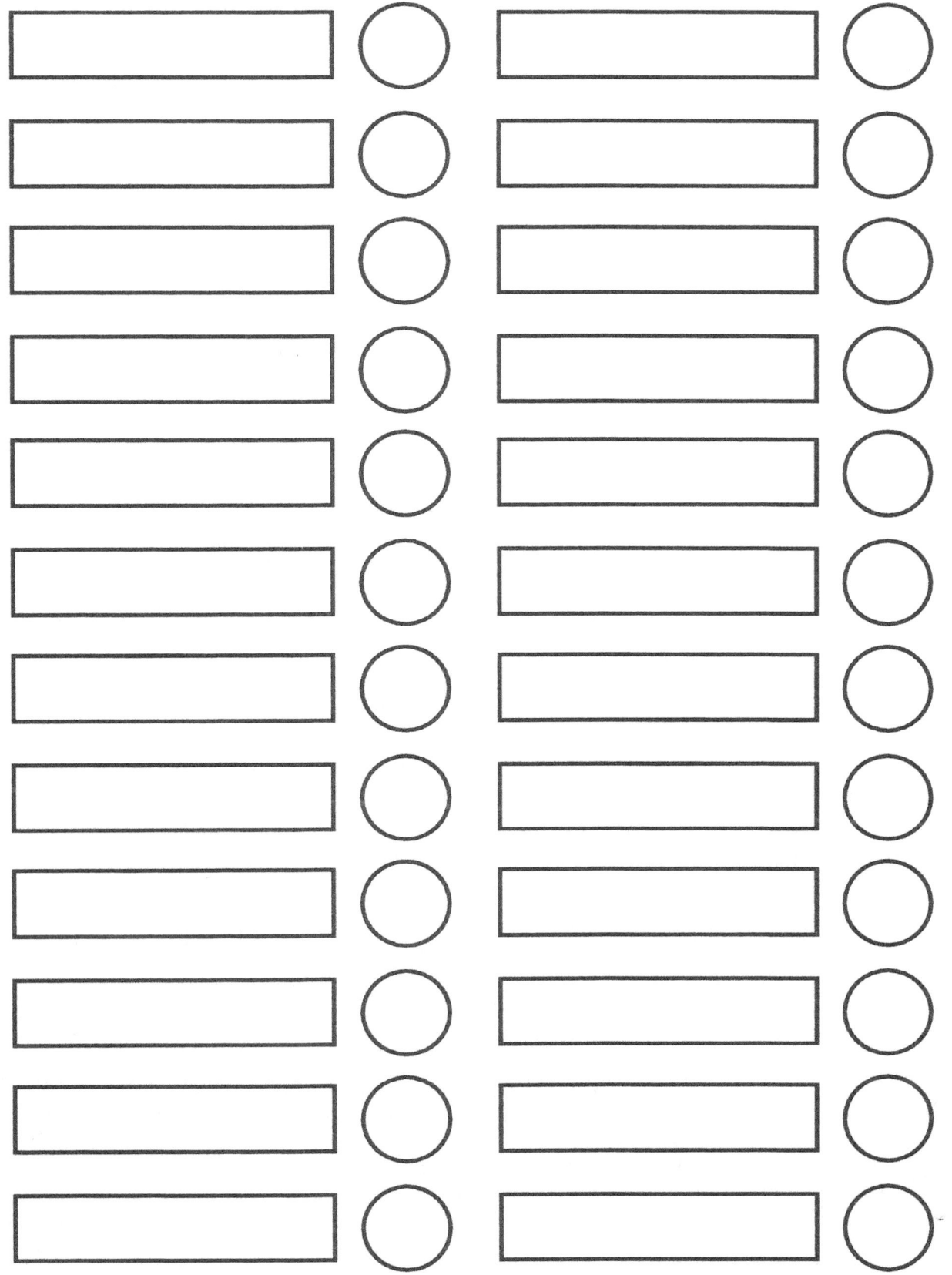

Protection Sheet

Remove from book

and insert between pages

when using markers.

Be sure to check out
our line of
digital prints & pdf coloring books
ready to download & color at:

https://www.etsy.com/shop/TwistedBranchStudios

www.ingramcontent.com/pod-product-compliance
Lightning Source LLC
Chambersburg PA
CBHW081059240526
45465CB00025B/2768